W9-BYI-151

DISCARDED
From the Nashville Public
Library

Property of
Nashville Public Library
615 Church St., Nashville, Tn. 37219

POT-BELLIED PIGS

WEIRD PETS

Lynn M. Stone

Rourke Publishing LLC
Vero Beach, Florida 32964

© 2002 Rourke Publishing LLC

All rights reserved. No part of this book may be reproduced or utilized in any form or by any means, electronic or mechanical including photocopying, recording, or by any information storage and retrieval system without permission in writing from the publisher.

www.rourkepublishing.com

PHOTO CREDITS:
All photos © Lynn M. Stone except page 12 © Norvia Behling

EDITORIAL SERVICES:
Pamela Schroeder

Library of Congress Cataloging-in-Publication Data

Stone, Lynn M.
    Pot bellied pigs / Lynn M. Stone
        p. cm — (Weird Pets)
    ISBN 1-58952-040-8
        1. Potbellied pigs as pets—Juvenile literature [1. Pot bellied pigs as pets.2. Pigs as pets. 3. Pets.] I. Title.

SF393.P74 S76 2001
636.4'85—dc21   00-054284

Printed in the USA

TABLE OF CONTENTS

POT-BELLIED PIGS

No one used to think of pigs as pets. In the 1980s that changed. Pigs began to live with families in their homes. It was a new idea. Some people thought pigs could be house pets.

These pig pets weren't big barnyard pigs. They were pot-bellied pigs.

Many pot-bellied pigs spend at least part of their day indoors.

Pot-bellied pigs are much smaller than normal American pig breeds, or kinds. Most adult pot-bellied pigs weigh just 125 to 150 pounds (57 to 68 kilograms).

Pot-bellied pigs are from Vietnam. They were first brought into Europe and North America in the 1960s. They weren't **imported** to be pets. They were used in **laboratories** and shown by zoos.

Pot-bellied pigs have small bodies but big voices to grunt and squeal.

In Vietnam, pot-bellied pigs are farm animals. They grow fat by eating rice, bran, and **aquatic**, or water-based, plants. The Vietnamese people raise pot-bellied pigs for the same reason American farmers raise pigs, for meat.

A pot-bellied pig has a body like an old couch. It has four short legs. Its back dips and its belly is low. Sometimes a pot-bellied pig's pot belly touches the ground!

Pot-bellied pigs travel very close to the ground.

POT-BELLIED PIGS: PET FRIENDLY?

Pot-bellied pigs are cute and they are almost cuddly. Does that mean they are good house pets?

Thousands of pot-bellied pig owners enjoy their pet pigs. Pot-bellied pigs are clean, smart, and good-natured. They can even be trained to use a litter box.

Like the family dog, pot-bellied pigs can learn commands, including "Sit!"

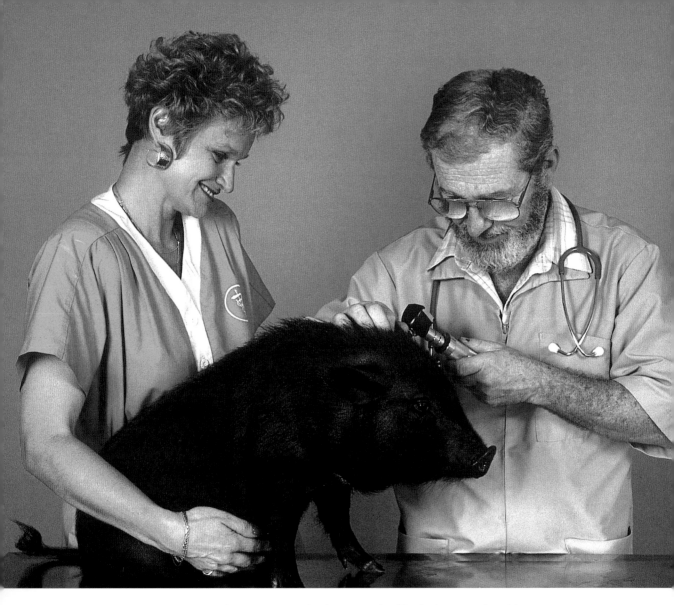

An animal doctor can help a pot-bellied pig stay healthy.

This pot-bellied pig and family dog get along well, but rescue groups say that dogs and pigs fight from time to time.

People who buy pot-bellied pigs often change their minds about keeping them. It's lucky that many animal **shelters** take pot-bellied pigs from unhappy owners. However, the shelters cannot keep all the pigs that are brought to them.

Why do so many owners give away their pet pigs? First, pigs are not indoor animals. Houses are not good homes for pigs. For example, pigs like to push their snouts into the ground to root for food. Indoor pigs may ruin carpeting and house plants. They may even eat parts of a house wall!

An outdoor life means a healthier, happier pig.

Another problem is that pigs are herd animals. As a pig grows older, it may fight with other pigs to decide who's "boss." It may even try to push people around. No one wants a pushy pet pig.

Owners can prevent some of these problems. One way is to keep the pigs outdoors most of the time. Owners should also keep at least two pigs. A pig won't be as bored if it has another pig for company.

A pot-bellied pig begins its morning walk from house to deck to yard.

CARING FOR POT-BELLIED PIGS

Pot-bellied pigs are **domestic**, or tame, animals. They need people to give them food, water, care, and shelter. That's a big job for the owner. A pot-bellied pig may live for 15 years!

Owners need to give their pet pigs outdoor space, at least some of the time. Anyone who can't do that should choose a different pet.

A child's plastic pool makes a good bathtub for a pot-bellied pig.

Outdoors, a pot-bellied pig needs to root, or dig, around in the ground. It also needs plenty of water to drink and to soak in. In very hot or cold weather the pig needs shelter. It needs a cool, shady summer shelter and a warm winter shelter.

A baby pot-bellied pig chows down on a breakfast of healthy food pellets.

FINDING A POT-BELLIED PIG

Breeders are people who raise and sell pot-bellied pigs. You can get a list of breeders from the North American Pot-Bellied Pig Association.

People who want pot-bellied pigs may go to a breeder or to an animal shelter. Shelters are always looking for good homes for pigs. Most shelters, however, will not give pot-bellied pigs to families with dogs or small children.

GLOSSARY

aquatic (eh KWAT ik) — living in water

breeder (BREED er) — a person who raises a kind of animal to sell to other people

domestic (deh MES tik) — refers to a type of animal that has been kept by people and tamed for hundreds of years, perhaps thousands

imported (im PORT ed) — brought into one country from another

laboratories (LAB rah towr eez) — places for scientists to study and experiment

shelter (SHEL ter) — a place where pets that need homes are cared for

INDEX

Further Reading

Stone, Lynn. *Pigs*. Rourke Publishing, 1990
Kelsey-Wood, Dennis. *Pot-Bellied Pigs*. Chelsea House, 1997

Websites To Visit

•www.petpigs.com   •www.pigs.org

About The Author

Lynn Stone is the author of over 400 children's books. He is a talented natural history photographer as well. Lynn, a former teacher, travels worldwide to photograph wildlife in their natural habitat.